FINISHING LINE PRESS

www.finishinglinepress.com

Quiet....

COLLECTED POEMS

poems by

Sauci Sharon Churchill
April 25, 1940 - June 3, 2011

edited by

Bruce R. Butterworth

Finishing Line Press
Georgetown, Kentucky

Quiet....

COLLECTED POEMS

ACKNOWLEDGMENTS

Numerous poems in *Running Down Division Street* (Finishing Line Press, 2004) and *A Red Fin*
(2007) first appeared in magazines and anthologies, among them, *Another Small Magazine,
Bitterroot, Bubbe Meisers Anthology, Centerpieces, Clark Street Review, Jewish Women's Literary
Annual, Metaphors, Poetica, Poetry Bone, Poetry Gallery, Rejected Quarterly, Slow Dancer, Stone
#13, Tapestries Anthology, Touching Quiet, Washington Review, Welcome Home.*

Publisher: Leah Huete de Maines
FLP Editor: Christen Kincaid
Cover Art: "THE ALCHEMIST'S GOLD" by Mindy Weisel
Author Photo: John Woo
Cover Design: Elizabeth Maines McCleavy

Order online: www.finishinglinepress.com
also available on amazon.com

Author inquiries and mail orders:
Finishing Line Press
PO Box 1626
Georgetown, Kentucky 40324
USA

This chapbook was made possible in part by donations to the ONE LAST WORD Program.
ONE LAST WORD helps to bring the last works of gifted poets to the world.

Contents

PART 4. *RUNNING DOWN DIVISION STREET (2004)*

PART 1: POEMS WRITTEN AFTER THE DIAGNOSIS OF ALS (IN NOVEMBER 2010)

Fluttering Into my poem

I was trying to write
on a grey afternoon

when I heard
a kind of scrabbling,
 then a slide and fall.
Something frantic
was conveyed.

Quiet

Sounds resumed
that didn't belong,
 a pinging
 softness on metal

On the screened porch,
 a small quivering thing
 cringed against the screen.

I propped the outside door
 turned quiet,
motionless.
A slight movement of air
and the touch of a wing

Quiet

That frightened sparrow
 could have been my heart

In Fear

in fear
my heart quakes
ice runs through veins
I am a handful of dust

Not an Ordinary Flicker

A bird at the feeder
its head a red shield
pecks away at suet
keeping other birds at bay

In *A Field Guide*
to Birds of North America
I find the *red bellied woodpecker*
male with scarlet nape and crown
small reddish tinge on his belly

In silhouette
the long beak
pecks voraciously
with jackhammer speed
suet disappears like
muscle from bone

each time I look,
nothing but the redhead
gorging on suet cake diminished

It casts a one-eyed glance my way
fear blossoms in my chest
spreading like blood in clear water

the striking beak,
the bright red head
I heed its call
a rolling chiv-chiv churrr

The Red Fox

I pull off weather stripping
(like John pulled out his IV)
charge through winter's door
into the snow world

inflating my lungs,
like a hot air balloon

I rise and then fall
dragged past the plane tree.
Straight as an arrow

I lay down
in the whitest of snow

later that evening
a small red fox
sniffs my face
and moves on

Not long for this world

the sicker I get
the less wine it takes
to turn me on
the skinnier I get
the more I'm told
to slather on the butter
have a milkshake every night
I have fallen in love with my bed
ever since the diagnosis
haven't worn my watch
I allow myself to skip my shower once a week
my old roommate said
you can't do this to me
you're supposed to be invincible
a terminal disease and you're in for soup

January: a wolf moon is howling and I howl along too

Respiration

The towering beech tree
whispered, sibilant
I take in your breath

Monkey man
cleats digging in
chain saw
swinging from his hip
stopping at each limb
long enough to lop it off

Tree-sized branches
tumble down
a hundred thousand
listening leaves
give off the last
of their life-giving oxygen
I am starved for the earth

The canopy
which sheltered us
from burning sun
  now a bright blue hole

Seduction

pure
white silky
scent of lavender
blush rose petals
scattered on linen

cradle of night

but wait
on close inspection
the bed is cluttered
with dozens of teeth
put there by a jinn
to ruin my sleep

I slide them into
a canvas bag
run to the river
throw it in the drink

and now
" to sleep, perchance to dream"

PART 2: POEMS (2007—OCTOBER 2010)

Our Lady of Angels

My Father commanded
  Dry the tears. Make a fist.
He struck the perfect boxer's pose
hands tight, muscles flexed
  Like this, swing out like this.
  next time they come, you'll punch.

Behind the backs of the good nuns,
Mary Ethyl and Carol Cadigan
conspired to play *crucifixion*
They sent me up our building's iron grate
climb up, they said, climb up little Jewgirl
you can be the one to put the nails in.

In Berkeley

Straight from Chicago, everything was a first.
My future husband shared a room with Doug O'Brien
A Murphy bed served as couch, table, bed
Yellow crud solidified on the dishes in the sink
When he wanted to eat, Doug scraped off a dish
as a seismologist, he always could feel
when unpaid bills were catching up with them
and they would leave in the dead of night
Their next place looked out to an alley
I cut squares of translucent paper for the windows
suffered from an overdose of hot buttered rum there,
please never mention it again

I walked to campus from my place on Benvenue Street
Peter, Paul, and Mary performed in the Rathskellar
Near the Carillon tower, Mario Savio orated
After marriage we moved to an apartment complex
like a cheap motel, which surrounded a turquoise pool
a flame burned from an ersatz torch 24/7
I washed my new husband's sweaters; the water turned black
I put my pony tail into a bun, went off to teach at Hayward High
where some of my students lived on the mudflats

We moved back to Berkeley to be closer to the physics lab
Our apt. had a kitchen nook and a lead lined flour drawer
when upstairs neighbors made love they sounded like a herd of elephants

Our landlord had been kicked out of rabbinical school
for radical ideas which we discussed long into the night
When I look back now I realize our life there was right nice

In the condominium garage

my father, heretofore known
as the Good Samaritan
leaned in to help a neighbor
whose woman had backed out
without opening their garage door

breached door gave way
landing on my father's inquiring head
a doctor put in a metal plate
we watched him filling up with blood
I asked the doctor what he would be like
if perchance he ever awakened

well, he won't be able to drive a car
Sir, from the looks of him
I doubt he will be able to tie his shoe

Dad died four days later
having spoken only the words
Get Dot before he left this world

Low Tide at Moss Beach

Wild sea today so
life guards plant red flags
along the shoreline

ankle deep in frigid water
we scoop for sea glass, green

our clothes are whipped against us
toes and aching knees are battered
by the punishing ocean tide

oblivious to the wind
a lemon sun licks
our skin to burning

every find is a triumph
why we want this glass
the reason is unknown

it shines a sly eye
from between wet pebbles
a sliver of our doing

The Very Disabled Woman

crippled by stroke
watched boats sail
in and out of the landing
each from a different place

words used to gush
from her mouth
honey smooth as
now her years run out

her world emptied
of what she loved
poetry skipped out on her
flew the coop

all through the night
bones click
telegraphing questions
where has all time gone?

Talisman

In her childhood keepsake box
she found a miniature Statue of Liberty,
the diminutive head of a dog
from a piece of children's jewelry,
heart shaped sea glass stones,
a tiny harmonica that still plays,
a bullet with a secret compartment

But her prize was liquid mercury
in a test tube stoppered with a rubber cap
She remembered handling the silvery substance

From the day Dr. Schwartz gave it to her
every trip to the dentist became occasion
to beg for more until she had a pea-sized glob

Today it's hazardous material
She turned in her thermometer
to the hazmat police, but did
not give up her quicksilver
which fractures and becomes
whole again in the lifeline of her palm

Dreams

to hear the night again
the lantern and the cricket

An older unclothed man
pressed against my bare chest
the pain was gone
he told me he had opened me up
and that he will keep it that way

cricket is captured in a stone lantern
carried carelessly by an old man
We let it out and I tell her
she will be released in one day
she does not complain
and I wonder why this seems to suit her

An Artful God

Leucojum
grow wild
on the banks
of the river Avon

at home
perched
on their stalks
the bell-shaped
flowers nod
each petal tinged
with a splash of green

As I Am

Who's to say on a shining summer evening
with my planet or star ascending
and my clothes strewn about
that I cannot dance
in the privacy of
the moon's light
just as I am
as I am

Resolutions

Here we sit
mid-January
and still we are not
healthier than before
We have not exercised or
traded animal flesh for soy

Haven't cleaned the closet
matched socks in the drawer
taken long walks with the dog

Because, baby, it's cold outside

That Girl

She would put on Mozart's Ninth
and her pink angora sweater
when she knew that he was coming

Augenblinck

When I was ten
my mother told me
I would bleed
   Blink
   Blink
I married under
a willow tree
divorced after 20 years
   Blink
my daughter is dressed
for her first day of school
then poised on a diving board,
she jumps, a bride glowing in white
her dog smuggled into the church
   Blink
I marry again in a courthouse
the Western Wall hears my prayer
In Venice I weep for beauty
in Bonaire I simply weep
   Blink
  Blink
My daughter remarries
in an ice blue sheath
no dogs at the country club
I am happy; my body whole
Blink I am missing a breast

There are deaths
(Dad's) ashes in the river
loneliness… regret
   Blink
Then comes a perfect birth
not the brilliant haloed one
but one for which
I gladly stake my claim

Phyllip, the boy next door

My best friend's sister Lorraine
slept with one arm above her head
to mimic a pin-up like Lana Turner
or Hedy Lamar just in case
someone should see her asleep

We used to have such dreamy dreams

We watched her kiss the boy next door
she in her magenta sweater with
white lace collar tacked on
he of the handsomest face

They were friends for life

He drank a special martini
cut her hair in his salon
where all the ladies loved him
He was true to his partner
of thirty-six years
until death did them part

O such dreamy dreams we had

From Russia

"Every man has a secret inside…" Mallarmé

Perhaps it was before
they boarded ship
that he fell in love
with her black braid
she with his blue eyes

*

When her diagnosis was new
grandmother told my mother
I'll teach you
to make gefilte fish
before I kick the bucket

Later as death approached
her face suggested
pain of concealment
My mother had always felt
something was left unsaid

*

Sixty years later
Cousin Florence
called to tell my mother
that she had a sister
    "Of course, Iris is my sister"

Not Iris, before your mother
married your father
she had a blue-eyed baby girl

The Billboard House

Few trees grew in our neighborhood
but there was a great billboard
in an empty lot on Crawford Avenue
or Pulaski Road depending on the year

We collected wood and cardboard boxes
but needed one lengthy board to put
across the struts behind the billboard

We antied up our pennies
walked to the lumberyard
with just enough for a single 2 x 4
which we carried between us like a trophy
hunters returning with meat for the tribe

It fit across the billboard beams
gave stability to our semi-secret playhouse

That night we were too excited to sleep
We ran, next morning, to our billboard house
which was awry, the 2 x 4 gone, and we knew
it had been taken by our landlord, Mr. Kurtz
We peeked through the storage window
next to his basement apartment and
sure enough there was our beautiful plank
    He denied that he had taken it
    told us we couldn't prove it and he was right

Memory

maybe I was four
the glint of the ring
in the crack between
the stone water fountain
and the cement sidewalk
near the wading pool   my ring
lost but amazingly found   by me

when my grandmother let me swim in the fountain

from Rumi program

I was raw
then I was cooked
then I was burned

read youngsters a poem—it doesn't have to be childlike
they "understand' in a deep way for
the old soul within has not yet been lost
still attached to the Source

a hundred years
before the earth be healed

more secrets

meeting up with Jacob and son at d'Vinci exhibition at National Geo
I knew what neither of them might never know
because the lady of the house talked in front of a maid,
assuming her to be deaf and invisible.
the secret trip to a gyn in Boston to remove one fetus of the twins

Fascination

I always took for granted
my father's interest in the salmon
never wondered what it meant

Both white and red men
are haunted by the salmon

Driven by their nature
salmon swim against the current
danger abounds on the
journey to their birthplace
salmon sharks and eagles
one in a thousand return to spawn

They swim past a place
on the McNeil River
where grizzlies wait
jousting for position
to snatch and eat them

Orphaned young,
with many sisters and brothers
Did my father long to return
to the homeplace before his loss?

Prose Piece

Something I had not thought of in years was brought to mind on p.17 of
Sag Harbor. It was a reference to passing a graveyard, "where custom called
for you to hold your breath no matter what you were, lest a spirit enter your
open mouth. Or so it was said." This brought me back to Chicago and high
school, when my friend Merle Gordon, brilliant and unique, would make a
drama of holding her breath as we rode the El past a cemetery. She never told
us why. Perhaps she did not know.

The Fireplug Unleashed

by older boys with a wrench
douses Division Street
water arcs sizzling pavement
and a dance of thrills ensues
shoes are kicked off ... tossed aside
soft tar is delicious underfoot

Before the water police arrive
icy sprays cool what was fiery red
fine droplets settle
on shades of sweaty skin
shrill voices scream
Hair flattens darkens clumps
or curls in spirals
whipping against eyes and faces
anger is drowned... submerged

In the evening after work
Adrienne's father in his undershirt
descends two flights of stairs
from a stifling apartment
mirror image of our own

Seating himself on the fireplug
clamped shut by *the authorities*
he resumes command of his corner
lights his habitual cigar

Out my bedroom window
I see him enveloped in potent smoke
guardian spirit of our neighborhood

Kiss (two versions)

When
food
or candy
dropped
to the ground
my mother taught me
Fehh, no good, throw it out
but Judy Derrick learned
a different and more practical lesson
Kiss it up to God and pop it in your mouth

When food or candy
dropped to the ground
my mother taught me
Fehh, no good, discard
but Judy Derrick learned
a different and more
practical lesson
Kiss it up to God
and pop it in your mouth

Disappearing

Big eared bats
accustomed to
eating juicy bugs
on the wing
do not thrive
in captivity
few are persuaded
to eat mealy worms

Easily stressed
they are subject
to *white nose syndrome*
a devastating fungal infestation

In summer dusk
I watch them pluck insects
from the soup of the air
In flight they are more
Balanchine than Balanchine

Up close those big ears
don't seem quite right
they live in dark places
our pulse pounds in fright

Help us to love them
Gather each spilled life
pass it through our hearts
sew it on like a button

Helen Thomas

My father was positively
so hurt by her comments
I cannot describe it
he called from California
did I know Helen Thomas?

Alyce and Streetcar Named Desire

In her last moments she said
I have always depended on the kindness of strangers
Those words cut me to the quick although
I believe they were meant for her husband

Alyce wept when
my husband and I separated
remembering, no doubt,
when her ex ran off with the au pair

We sometimes drank tea together
each from our own blue willow cup

When the jockey statue disappeared
from my next door neighbor's lawn
on Martin Luther King's birthday
they assumed I was responsible
When a fellow I dated arrived in a pick-up
Alyce called to make sure I was all right

Her second husband, crippled by a wave,
had to give up his medical practice
He killed spiders and emptied mouse traps
He tied himself to a tree in order to
mow the steep bank of his front lawn

When Alyce told me she had ovarian cancer
she showed me her photograph at the beach
wearing a big hat, looking for all the world
like Jeanne Moreau

Near the end of her time
She asked me to help change her position
which her husband to spare me discouraged
because of the smell but I got her comfortable
then patted her leg
She stared at her husband and that's when she
said that thing about the kindness of strangers
An hour later he called to tell me she was dead

I always drink tea
from my blue willow cup
and sometimes I think about Alyce

Our first time he said

Explore me
Oy
this is maybe something new
So I nosed about
and I guess it worked
because I am married
to the man in the hat

A Husband Who Loves Condiments

record snowfall
equivalent weight
of African elephant
on the rooftop
broken branches
power failures
ice dams and
sagging gutters

we're out of milk
low on toilet paper
downed trees
on power lines
snow plows stuck
on arteries
government closed
school out all week
harried parents
thinking harikari

we dig patches
so dogs have
a place to poop
inside temp
hovers at 55
we suffer roof leaks
no Washington Post
for one long week

We long for fresh greens
and meds are running low
cough syrup's gone
no crossword
minds rot
my husband comments
We're out of Grey Poupon

Barn Swallows

Shredded plastic bags wave
from their ramshackle nests
but nothing stops the swallows

In my twenties
after giving up a hank of bowel
the good doctor admonished me
  hang on to your sense of humor
  colostomy's not the end of the world

In my fifties
I traded my left breast for life
nothing funny about it
more than a decade has passed
I see dark humor in my reflection
And still, the barn swallows fly

Hi Ho Silver, Away

Like your shadow
pain does not twist off,
it builds like fire
on a bone-dry day.

Washed in the moon's brightness
pain, like the night sky, is vast.
Twinkling, it seems to come and go
but is steadfast as the North Star

Power Outage

Forecast to cause damage, the wind roars
Oak and hickories sway
Nations of birds swarm the feeder

Unplugged, in darkness once more
hanging like a prism to capture light
I am hopeful but incapable of choosing

I never had religion but
revered the fine grain of wood
polished it with my soft rag to shine

After the storm
I am carved out like a pumpkin
the meanness inside scooped clean.

Asian Carp

Asian carp
grow 4 feet long
weigh 100 pounds

In Chicago
to slow their advance
the locks open less frequently

If I don't open my door
can I make sure
no bad comes in

EgyptAir Flight 990

A call rips the night
the director for aviation security operations for the country howls,
digs another chunk from his thumb
then appears at the command center, deadly calm.

A moth, wings outstretched,
spins in a carafe of ice water
the air is sticky with webs
as fast as we clear them, spiders rebuild

After the briefing nobody says the word *bomb*.

*

When elephants are lost from each other
a fluttering begins under the skin of their forehead
they send out a contact call
chanting interrogatory rumbles

If an elephant goes down
the others sing to keep its spirit up
       and then they try to raise it.

How Like a Serpent

The drone of a leaf blower
charms *ceratostigma plumbaginoides*
to send up a stalk with a flower
so startlingly blue, the eye blinks,
can't go wide enough to take it in

The sound of an outboard motor
as my parents' fish Lake Marie
I try to sleep on the way home
trying not to hear the wet slap
of gasping sunfish and bluegills
on the floor of the old Chevrolet.

My Father

My Father In a shoebox lined with cotton
his birth and death both premature

A bolt gave way
the cable flew
with all its tensile strength
It found him like a missile
smashed his boy scout head

Nothing could stop his Precious Blood
And he became not-my-Father
a stranger in a hospital bed
pie-faced, shaved, cologned
Afraid I was that he'd wake up the way he was

Dipping his ashes into the moving river
I watched as they disappeared in a swirling plume

First Time in Paris

A tiny Frenchwoman
in a flowered dress
and high heel shoes
heaves our luggage
into the trunk of her cab.
We share the back seat
with her old black poodles
who smell.
She drives at breakneck speed
to a darkened hotel in Montparnasse
We awake to the sound of coughing,
the smell of chocolate and cigarette smoke.

Bookstalls unfold along the Seine
whose dark metallic smell
settles around our neck and shoulders.
Pont Neuf, hidden in shadows, is wrapped.
Domes emerge and the city begins to dazzle.

We walk streets that feel endless
searching for a man you once lived with.
His name is still on a door but there is no answer.

Breast Cancer Maven

My mother had a bad year
First my father got bopped on the head
Then her daughter lost a breast

At her 80th birthday bash
Second and third cousins
On my mother's side
Not seen for thirty years
Clustered about me
BRCA 1's and BRCA 2's
Hands over their scars
Still here after 30 years
to encourage me

I was pulled out of their circle by my old friend
Who said "Don't become the breast cancer maven"

intaglio

Everything extraneous
 has been cut away
I am inked
ready to be printed

Drape yourself upon me
 like damp paper
Take my imprint
I am the plate

Puppy Summer

Either someone poisoned the dog or it ate rat poison.
At first, we thought it howled because of the storm
or because it was caught between two porch slats
but when my father arrived, he knew the dog was dying,
that she had given birth to pups and he took her away.

Next morning, we found the puppies at the Chinese Hand Laundry.
Turns out, it was the Chinaman's dog. So that summer, I had a purpose:
feeding the hungry pups' eyedroppers of milk and karo syrup.
The Chinaman didn't seem to mind a bunch of neighborhood kids
invading his shop. We stayed mostly in the back, supervising
each other while he worked up front, ironing shirts that smelled burnt.

I arrived at his steamy shop early each morning.
He would be frying delicious smelling pork chops in an iron skillet
and with gesture, always offered me some. I longed for a taste
but my mother made me promise not to eat his food.
I never saw him eat what I brought, not even a piece of birthday cake.

We named the pups; my favorite, Johnny, had light brown spots.
We didn't much like the plain white ones but dutifully gave them names
like Pinky and Jane and we fed them, too, through an endless summer.

A sofa occupied the space where the Chinaman ironed but I never saw him rest.
A dazzling sheet covered an old sofa where we played with the pups as he worked.
He never seemed to mind when one of the puppies peed.
His bed was separated from the front of the shop by one of his blinding white sheets
suspended from a string. He had a trunk, a piece of real jade, a photograph of his
wife, and us.

One morning he was gone.
All of the puppies were gone.
An ugly man I could not understand
was scaping Rose *Lee Chinese Hand Laundry*
from the window glass, substituting his own unwelcome name.

Do Not Walk Across the Lunar Lawn

A woman gathers food and herbs
What she cannot carry
she wraps into her hair
Radiant as a tree her ruby
leaves fall opening the space

Over the ocean an airplane flies the night sky
its lights are on when it goes down
A disembodied Louis Armstrong song
plays somewhere across the water.
Beyond lies a cemetery where blue lights shine
and chrysanthemum smells pungent, earthy, fecal.

There was a peach glow
The night of the lunar eclipse
The night her father was made to dust
His face smiled wide as the sycamore
Wide as the wind between fields
We reach across space once filled with stars.

All Good Things Come in Pears—Pear Council

I got the bruise in the night
I 'm the hostess with moroseness
I wonder where the yellow went
and why the heathen rage

My daughter says I have a flubby bottom
Nothing bears close scrutiny these days

Edgar Bergen had Charley
McCarthy and Mortimer Snerd
All good things come in pairs

Collect the pear and heart shapes
crescent shells and moons
I am told at hush of twilight
seashells jingle in the tides.

My Zaida and Morgan Freeman

appear in a dream
what they have in common
may never be known
the two of them converse
in a corner of my kitchen
Zaida asking for a little more coffee

a soft spring rain begins to fall
there is a sound of running water
like an upstairs shower running full blast
water pounds harder and louder

light thickens and an acrid smell pervades
dangerous light flashes yellow-green
puffs of concrete sprout from the ceiling
like a chalky cloud of dust
the air gets thick and hard to breathe
hairline cracks appear in the plaster
droplets bead along the seams
moisture sweats from painted surfaces
cracks enlarge: old paint starts to blister

rubble starts to fall
the ceiling crashes down
hunks of steaming plaster
settle into broken silence

Elizabeth Taylor, archetypal star goddess, I am not

Mother, mother
is all I ever hear
My brood surrounds me
when trouble is near

each has a hold of
a piece of my clothing
an arm or a leg
or the bulge of my belly

my breasts are laden
with life giving milk
my clothes stained yellow,
throw up on silk

bra straps cut hard
into my shoulders
indentations deepen
as I grow older

I am lauded by
all sorts of folks
One said to my face
I was archetypal
don't know what it means
don't like how it sounds
maybe it's something
to do with my cycle

once in a while
when I look at my kids
part of me yearns to
scrap reputation
slap each naughty bottom
without hesitation

Would someone read my silly verse? thanks

Fishing For Blues

The thin man disappears at the chest
into wide waders
Foreshortened, he strides into the sea
A smell of marshmallows
emanates from about his face and mouth
his pipe's a black scar

An arm and fish line arcs above the ocean
attaching to the sky
The pole quivers and he watches for a strike

Mullet melt and the sun starts down
Our shadows stretch away from us
pulling against our earthly bodies
Squirming to get comfortable in the sand
right side lumpy, left side falling
into a hole where my breast had been

Shoes from Next-to-New

Italian
two-tone
ivory and tan
wing-tipped and beautiful
a good-sized heel to make you tall
and
a straw hat that hid your face in lacy shadow

The Toys of Childhood

Jacks
roller skates
 a small red ball
a slate board
maybe a yoyo
my teddy bear
Butch

Inspired by manly hunter Theodore Roosevelt
 who refused to shoot for sport an injured bear

Named for Butch Whitney
whose family owned the first TV
at 6 P.M. we kids descended
 upon their darkened living room
to cluster before the round Zenith eye
that held Kukla, Fran and Ollie

But with B**utch**,
I can almost remember
the orgiastic moment
 when I bit off his tongue
the dusty taste of dry red felt
 lingering in my mouth

PART 3. *A RED FIN* (2007)

Off Kilter

Bucky filled our lives
with her good hound smell
the little brown dog slept
in my daughter's bed
a pillow for their heads
Bucky this and Buckwheat that
Buck from the pound grew plump with us
                    and then grew lean

                    *

Wisteria snaked up and down the oak tree
around gateposts, suturing them shut
That stranglehold could take a wall down
                    and yet
they woke me to see the northern lights
let me play in a fountain with tritons
let me pick a scallion from a victory garden
rubbed off the dirt with thick warm hands
                    gave me the shining bulb

                    *

Three new moons orbit Neptune, all of them off kilter

In my garden the mourning dove
still in death, the bird,
still the glassy eye, still the vent

In Guadeloupe my dress billowed out around me
airborne above dark shapes, I looked down to see a red fin

I lick the place between the devil and my mother's voice
shake hands with fire and my heart is burned
something precious fills both cupped hands
Shattered, it holds together like a puzzle

Rejection Slips

"Ammonites" is too long
"Nitinol": same problem
I like the concept of "In the Yukon"
but it's not a poem
likewise "$189 Worth of Power Tools"

"The House a Cloud Passed Through"
makes me say *so what*
I like "Red" especially the last line
but I need to know more

I admire your pluck

Red

Red is dying,
yet everything looks the same.
Not a leaf stops its cycle in deference.
The sun beats feverishly on his slate roof.
Only his dog has ceased to bark,
as if to say, under the circumstance,
let children play where they choose.

Waiting

After surgery's unnatural sleep
from which I had not planned to wake
someone whispered in my ear
"a simple rearrangement....the body adapts."

Soup cools and a layer of fat clouds over
words skim the surface
tilt the world and they slide off like teeth or nails.

When you go deep into your life
is it sand there and I am the sea?
Or is it sea and I the foam
crusting at water's edge
dry where once I glistened?

Drinking coffee in my kitchen in the evening
in pale light dreaming backward now that I'm old
I remember when a bird got caught like some dark thought
and feathers scraped the wall like metal spoons.

Now I mount the glossy bird
part the feathers
throw my arms around the throbbing neck
a red eye looks my way.

Patched Cloth

I. Rachael

I hear the tread of her bare feet
padding along the rim of memory
she smells of soap flakes and wax

2. The birthday cake

On my tenth birthday
my mother told me
I would bleed

My hand trembled
around the knife and
spoiled red sugar roses

3. A limp from shrapnel

To my uncle in the army
we sent great looped salamis
he brought back rayon scarves
embroidered with fuchsia flowers
the word *Capri* and a purple heart

4. California years

Dawn came
dripping and gray
foghorns breaking morning
into manageable parts

Leather sandaled
days went by
through groves of
Eucalyptus trees

5. Dark union

We listen to night sounds
flannelled and wooled
against the cold
unaware of our grave mission

6. The couple

Dusk fills the room
as sand fills a bottle

What they do not say
rests like a hundred year egg
between them

7. The end

Lived with a man
seventeen years
didn't know till
the day he left
he hated Sundays

Hunter's Moon

Perch jump onto the lines of fisher boys
who watch us move against each other
wide-eyed as the bluefish
that plunk their bodies
against the molten water
Night gets red and you can taste the glow
fire shoots across the water
capturing light not dreamed of

Two men chased by moonlight
struggle with a five gallon can
filled with suns and spots and splashing blues

Lanterns blossom on the bridge
but the light is struck from
within the skin of dreamers
calling the silver fins towards them
luring them into their darkening buckets

My Roommate at Berkeley

Helene was courted by the son of a Greek Orthodox priest
who spoke no English but made it known that she looked like Nefertiti
or Elizabeth Taylor done up as Cleopatra for a Time magazine cover.

He was her first...boyfriend, everything.
She loved the way his trousers blossomed up
when they made love
        in poison ivy once at the arboretum.

Theophanes became our night visitor
in the space partitioned by our landlady
who turned her attic into three apartments
on Benvenue Street, walking distance to campus.
Our largest room was a commodious bath with a footed tub
        where Helene once spent a week in baking soda.

They spent their nights on the sofa
a Greek-English dictionary in arm's reach
awed by how easily male and female slipped together.

          *

Their marriage was kept secret
their room too terrible to show.
He ate at meal jobs, brought her scraps.
When life came to her belly
she said that she felt nothing.

Helene dressed carefully
for Kennedy's Bay of Pigs speech
she said *Today I am a ragamuffin*

In the spring she vowed never to shave her armpits.
She danced in circles at noon wearing
a red peasant blouse, tossing her glossy black hair.
Helene, where are you now, how are you dressed,
are there scars where you scratched yourself bloody?

C&O Canal at Seneca

A young man,
the scarf at his throat a red slash,
offers reefer to a matron
walking the canal
to flush cobwebs
from her brain.
 "Mary Wanna?"
Her eyes widen.
 "What you some kind
   tree-watch person?"

She takes a trembly breath
turns away without a word

                    *

A man and his ten year old son
squirrel hunting near Riley's Lock,
spot a skull on a wool blanket

The incident is reported
to the game warden
who notifies the police

State medical examiners
view dental charts
of a county woman
missing since August
to determine whether they
match the skull's dentures.
No foul play is suspected.

                    *

The woman
reading this account in the *Washington Post*
draws a sudden breath and bares her teeth.

The Old Drive-In Movie

A whir of wings cools the air
feathers on every surface soften the edges
hear the soothing coo of roosting doves
whose droppings frost the old projector
the unspooling reels.

I remember a little black kid
on an *EL* platform in Chicago
who dropped his bag of peanuts.
When pigeons approached boldly
he cried out *eye eye* and I surmised
it was the birds' red eye that terrified

The drive-in's now defunct
overrun with birds.
We scavenge
behind the crumbling screen
breathing dry guano air
holding each other
because we know
that soon something
with a crimson eye
will scan our bones
and wonder at our neon relics

Red Cherries in a Crystal Bowl

I know
a potter
who makes
covered jars
so he may
look inside
and find the secret

There are
new cracks
in the crystal bowl
but darkness
has been pierced
like the shell
of an egg
and light has found
new ways to enter

A Baffling Reality

Front Page:
The father of a kidnapped girl in Baghdad pleads
Shine a red hot bead of light wherever she goes

Obituary:
Cause of death was nitrogen narcosis, rapture of the deep

Local:
Chanting saves life of leopard at the Washington Zoo

Crime:
Trail of tootsie rolls leads police to burglar

Human Interest:
Hobo colony lives mole-like
amid inferno of pipes beneath Park Avenue

Science:
An iceberg drifts toward Africa with a colony of penguins.
Beavers weave a bag of large bills stolen from a casino
into their dam on a creek in eastern Louisiana

Op-Ed:
After 30 years in a cave
Onada, a Samurai, emerged into a baffling reality
I thought my orders were forever

"I thought it would take a silver bullet . . . ." Julius Hobson

After cancer takes a bite
night terrors crowd the bedroom
phantoms whisper *time is short*
the mind cannot sleep
you practice your farewells and
divide your earthly possessions.

Cancer tweaks you toward religion.
Shadows flair in vapor lights,
appliances hum and the computer,
benign or malignant, flashes its red eye.

It is not the ending but an overlong third act
It is not the light at the end   but the tunnel
with its smell of wet concrete and urine
webs left behind by the hunter,
prey swaddled like babies
awaiting the hungry spider.

A melodrama after all
        though it leans
             towards something better.

Cool hands cradle a feverish brow
Something flutters in the gloom
soft against raw skin
There is mercy in the seedpods
studding the stem of wild hyacinth.

Five Days in Jamaica

For Bruce

(1)

At the airport men drift by
offering ganja in subliminal voices
our arms dangle like white sticks
our saucer eyes belong to lovers
Everything we see thrills us

Land crabs move away as we approach our destination
beautiful Jamaican girls braid the hair of American women
who are told they look like Bo Derek
The hotel offers fresh mango juice,
a clean white room that faces out to water,
hand-sewn sachets of fresh herbs on our pillows.

Guests wear white shoes with matching belts
call everyone *boy* or *mon* in booming American voices

(2)

Next morning we ride a bus to market
where we see ackee and sugar cane
Machetes chop the tops off coconuts
We drink the milk, photograph silverblue fish in wooden boxes,
walk among old men gossiping and take pictures which still haunt us
Small children in brown uniforms stick to us like glue, begging

(3)

Saturday we drive through rain on rutted roads
Women flag us down, jump into our car to warn us
of men and tell us how little this island offers their sons

(4)

Sunday we drive into the mountains where coffee grows
Children slow us down to touch us
In the trees, bananas are wrapped in blue plastic...
something about ripening

We leave the car on a jungle road to walk in opposite directions
Suddenly a missile fells me, my face is on fire
out of nowhere a man with a machete appears, helps me to my feet
you've been hit by a coconut, you'll be ok, I'll get some ice
my nose and lips swell to outlandish proportion
my lover takes the coconut as a souvenir

.

We drive the coastal route, stop at a Rastafarian's cooking fire
Hinting we'd like some fish, we make a deal
Seated on an overturned boat
we eat delicious little bony fishes from the pan
Later we drink Red Stripe at a stand off the side of the road.
That night rhythmic drumming draws us to a street fair
where lights and food and reggae music
and a moon just slightly out of round, gentles the air around us
Photos show our arms falling gracefully along the curve of our bodies

(5)

Finding the roads undriveable
we return the car to concentrate on water
At the reef you suddenly bend and fold
dive down to swim amid watery roses, green quiet
through the *glas botem* boat, sundappled, you are beautiful

At Rick's Place in Negril, I descend a rock ladder,
submerge my face and mask until the world disappears
I am in a quiet wavy place listening to clicking noises
Iridescent cuttlefish and a vast school of blue tang
dart as one in a swirl around us

In Croatia

Above a fort that housed prisoners
a Croatian flag cracks in the wind
In the Krajina, houses pocked with bullet holes,
have red numbers designating Serb or Croat
We can almost smell the smoke
My husband cannot stop photographing
one bombed-out house after another

At a table outside a café we watch Saturday men
talking softly in language we cannot understand
Nobody stares but we are marked as tourists

A General known for war crimes
smiles from well-placed billboards.
At a village bar, his picture
is propped against a bottle of grappa.
Rumors say he's protected by Jesuits

                    *

In Rijeka our friend Srecko grills fish in the living room fire stove,
Tatyana bakes coffeecake for breakfast, explains the currency.
They take us to the mother-of-all-caves in Slovenia.

Above a restaurant, their son Luka's room overlooks the sea.
He says fishing nets are draped for photo ops
We visit a tiny shop, select seafood from the morning catch.
Descending to a smoky basement room, we perch on rickety benches,
order wine, and wait for lunch of tiny finger fish, squid

At the seaside we set up the tripod.
Back home, looking at photographs, we see
the smoke of my husband's pipe reflecting sunlight

Smoke

after the door is locked
women gather in a circle of chairs
in the middle, a wool blanket
on it: a shell, a sage bundle, a feather

an elder wearing soft red shoes
cradles burning sage in an abalone shell
moves soundlessly around the circle
blowing smoke towards every woman
each pulls the smoke to her face
pushes it over her head
turns around for completion

another elder follows
touching every woman with the eagle feather

when all are blessed, she holds the talking stick
explains that nothing spoken may leave this room

a smoke serpent roams the air
the stick, wrapped in twine
with a dangling eagle feather
is passed woman to woman

with the stick in her hand
each leans into the circle,
takes a breath to speak of loneliness
unborn children, lost grandmothers
afterwards each woman hugs every other

when the door is opened no one moves to leave

The Couple at Quaker Meeting

My husband is afraid of dying
so we search for a creed
that doesn't scare him half to death
with promises of everlasting torment

In a large bright room of pleasing proportion
bench seats are padded to ease the long sit

Some nod as if agreeing with themselves,
some nod off. Amid beatific countenances
a few smiles are angled toward heaven or the oak tree
people stare out the window or run fingers through their hair
a man rises and natters on about his colleagues
who are not Quaker but capable of good

In a room silent but not empty
they meditate   or not.
dust motes like tiny stars
punctuate an infant's gurgle

Congregants dress plainly with some exceptions.
In front of the couple a young woman
wears fluffy red braids like Raggedy Ann
Her arm sports a sinuous tattoo.
My husband hunches forward,
his back a smooth letter "C"
drawn perhaps to the hypnotic arm
or trying to breathe her scent

Duct to the Heart

You opened
petal by petal
your hand held my heart
til the trembling stopped
your eyes burned with knowing

Imagine an angle of pain
pressing in like torn tin
imagine
the smell of wet windowsills
open for the rain, open for love

blood clots my creamy wool
I am the lamb, gathered in

In Dreams

my husbands
become a composite
of their worst traits

night visitors
sit on my chest
unceremoniously
poke open my red eyes

phantasmagoric tales
disappear with the dawn
life seeps through shut lids

I'm losing my stuffing
          my stuff

washed in the moon's brightness
 poems blossom
          like night flowers
when dreaming gives way to light
I am left groping for wisps

if I could be tapped like a maple
 sap running
          gorgeous and sweet
I would read the hieroglyphics
thrown onto the gathering snow

The Undoing

a film of
destruction
runs backward
on a spindle

broken things
become whole
as in beginnings

rivers of blood
flow back into
wounds

wine back to water
clear water again

PART 4: *RUNNING DOWN DIVISION STREET* (2004)

Herbie's Fish Store: Chicago

I.

With the Sabbath coming on
in the old place on 16th
Aunt Gert waved a chopping knife
women came for carp and whiting
bones and heads to make gefilte fish

My pregnant mother was hired
to wrap fillets in butcher paper
juices splattered
sweetness filled the air
she was dotted luminous with scales

II.

Lassie guards the new store
Herbie lifts us onto the strong dog's back
with his talented fisherman hands
my cousin Lowen and I hold to soft brown fur
our eyes ablaze afraid of one wrong move
steadied by the smell of fresh fish

III.

When my cousin is thirteen
his father dies and Gertie
still stirring a cauldron of fish heads
gives him the job of making horseradish
tears roll down his cheeks as
he grates the bitter root against a wheel

Making Wine on Division Street
1945

In a corner of the bedroom
grapes bubbled in a crock
a wasp buzzed mad for the juice
a sign for Trucko's tavern blinked all night
And me in my bed full of dreams
guilty my hand wet from touching
mom dad me and a bushel of grapes fermenting
we breathed the winey air

Heat knocked through the pipes
melting my pink rubber pig to the radiator
All the years I watched that stain

My father built a radio cabinet
the black lacquer surface smooth as glass
four doors were inlaid with ivory
one opened to a square of woven silk
stretched on a frame to hide the speaker

Let's Pretend and The Shadow Knows
emerged from dragons' mouths and lotus flowers
silk threads were frayed from my touch
I crouched before the radio listening for a sign

*

the yellow chair
was my reading place
Its contours fit me perfectly.

I traced patterns on a brass vase
filled with chopsticks
my hands smelled dirty, metallic
I played in front of the in-a-door bed
where my grandmother slept
tried not to notice her grimace of pain
after she died Zaida talked to himself
at night he'd set his truss on the yellow chair
my mother did not explain what it was for

Mother made drapes, the fabric printed with
willow trees, Japanese maidens holding fans
red, chartreuse and forest green to match the walls

My friends thought our flat exotic
from a window we watched rats
run between buildings
During blackouts we pulled the shade

JoAnn said she saw God
but we didn't believe her
Larry Greenfield's sister
slept with a pillow between her legs
We plundered our parents' drawers for clues

Jealous of Adrienne's older sister
with her maroon sweater and pointy breasts
we spied on her and Phillip
to learn things we didn't know

Adrienne's father called me *Cerise*
Evenings found him sitting on the fireplug
at the corner of Division and Harding
chewing his cigar
arms folded across his chest
waiting for the smoke to clear

Running Down Division Street

Slammed the door
that separated
me from Jerry Lyon
He called me dirty Jew
I kicked him in the groin
He roared revenge
became homosexual
for spite.

Once inside
I flicked the lights
avoiding thought of
the in-a-door bed
where my grand-
mother died.

The doctor lived
one flight down
would not come up
he'd had his bath
he'd catch his death.

I banged the radiator
with a hammer
all day long
to let him know
when she was dead.

We found
a plate
of hard-
boiled eggs
at our front door.

Old West Side: Chicago

Horses clop down the alley
from his wagon a fruit peddler cries
Water malone, watermalone

Two children on a third floor porch
watch headless chickens run in circles
in the butcher's backyard
They spit watermelon seeds over the
blistering rail *"bombs over Tokyo"*

Old men in black build a *sukkah*
Fruit dangles from strings
They spend their evenings beneath
the plywood slats
harvesting their memories
remembering inaccessible fields

Aunt Iris' Wedding

The Rabbi was late
The little flower girl
could not be persuaded down the aisle.
The old ones had their schnapps
and someone lost false teeth in a potted plant.

Irresistible in pale pink tulle,
the flower girl was passed above the table,
passed among the uncles over spilled food and
blood red wine by hands that grabbed and pinched
in admiration.

She was spun like cotton candy
from Uncle Julius to Uncle Max.
Above the flames of a candelabrum
her faery dress caught like tinder
melting the diaphanous net,
until the hands of her father found her,
smothered the flames against his chest.

Streetcar to North Avenue Beach

Bathing suits itched and pinched beneath our clothing
Sweat frayed the transfers and tattooed numbers on our palms
We smelled the fumes of August
Lake Michigan seemed light years away

Our heads filled with water dreams,
We crossed the sudsy Chicago River
White with Ivory Snow.

At the beach
waves moved us like chessmen
tiny shells washed into our suits
My top never covered my nipples.
Old ladies watched from aluminum chairs
planted in sand at the water's edge

Kids kicked up the burning sand
Running in pain to reach the water
eager beyond pain, like we were,
watching the older ones courting

As We Gather In Our Mothers' Kitchens

Fill the cellar
with roots and wine,
bring in sun warm stones
to place around the hearth
I want a reservoir of earth
beneath my fingernails for
when the winter comes.

Days grow short,
with schools and shoes,
preserves and bulbs,
and lengthening shadows.
Hands are busy making ready
and the day is filled with filling
mouths and jars and cookies and
the ice cream man twinkles off
to warmer climes.

twigs snap
leaves and fires crackle
hear the apple bites

The pantry grows
pickles green and briny.
The basement harbors dandelion wine.
The tubers are cautioned not to trouble
themselves with roots; I kiss each eye.

Night Out

Leaning on the freezer
men with wooden spoons
scoop butter brickle

Sara Lee lurks
in the background
wearing tap pants

She thinks
it strange
to see grown men
eating ice cream
with little sticks

Three delinquents
with a taste
for the exotic
suck oysters
out of tins
oil greases
their chins

They move
quickly
from the
open tins
smelling fishy

Pegged Pants, Cigarettes and Knives

My father was a maker of knives, keeper of the knife
I purchased mine next door to Livia's pizzeria
There were wooden booths and red vinyl stools
And comic books under the counter and
Josephine's beautiful sisters who talked to us

In the basement were loaves for sausage sandwiches
and huge rounds of cheese to be scraped of mold
and a scale to weigh out rounds of pizza dough

The ovens were fired up 4 o'clock sharp
And I ate there nights my parents worked
After dark I ran with all my strength
from that warm place
ran home heart beating wildly
past the newsstand past the bully boys
pounding uncarpeted stairs to the second floor
where the door trembled loose in the doorjamb
and I could open it with my knife

Jenny and Mike's Pizzeria

Years later
her mouth remembers
the blackened crust
sausage a little spicy

Sheltered in a dark stained booth
a sour yeasty smell prevailed
men drank beer along the bar
her parents let the little girl in a pinafore
siphon foam from their glasses

Her mother offers a triangle of pizza
lifted high enough to sever tentacles
of cheese that could smack her in the face
she opens eager like a baby bird
for a taste that blisters the roof of her mouth

Books and the Dark Behind Them

I.

In an old bookcase bought from strangers
I found Victor Hugo's Toilers of the Sea
with gold tooled letters and designs
I had just learned longhand writing
copied words into a notebook
 equinox, parapet, archipelago

II.

Compton's Picture Encyclopedia
had tinted color plates:
lily pads a man could stand on
lemmings marching into the sea
Ubangi women with enlarged lower lips
Longfellow's "Hiawatha"
    By the shining big sea waters
    Stood the wigwam of Nokomis
    Daughter of the moon...

III.

My father's boy scout manual was
bound by his hand for a merit badge
pages tissue paper thin
    how to survive lost in the forest,
    how to snare small animals,
    make fire without flint and steel,
    treat wounds that don't bleed freely.

A Bond in My Name

My grandfather sewed pockets
for Hart, Schaffner and Marks
belonged to the union and when
I was seven I went to their camp
where you had to drink water
when you ate meat.

When my grandmother died
at age fifty-three
Zaida moved in with us
got old and sloppy
went around in his shorts
saying over and over
my grandmother's name.
"Sima sima SIMA, Oy Gevaldt."

When he retired
they called him to picket
He struck with the others
in front of the menswear
on Morse Avenue, northside Chicago
He made a few dollars
spent time with his cronies.

After his death just a week at the most
a check came to me from a bond in my name
signed by his union, the Workmen's' Circle
I bought this ring with the hundred and twenty
set with three opals in a small circle
and it's from my Zaida who took me, but rarely
to what he called Farfel, the beach in Chicago.

A Limp from Shrapnel

To my uncle in the army
we sent great looped salamis
he brought back rayon scarves
embroidered with fuchsia flowers
the word "Capri" and a purple heart.

Hospital: Southside Chicago

My room had a metal bed
a worn brown vinyl chair
Hector's sister asked
"Don't you wish you lived in a room like this?"

I asked what Hector ate.
Eight, he looked like six.
"Cokes and candy bars
he cries a lot
Our mother gives him soda to make him stop."

His mother visited every day
in iridescent green taffeta
the color of a Japanese beetle

Swaddled in diapers
Hector sat on my lap while
friendly nurses frowned.
One night their screaming woke me
There was whispered talk of worms so long,
so long like this and I was told never,
no never hold Hector on my lap again.

In a dream of that time,
the good Dr. Ramirez,
In beautifully articulated Spanish,
explains about nutrition to Hector's mother
offers the telephone number of a social worker
explains that more than coke must wash the
black stubs that pass for teeth in the mouth of little Hector
instead of "See ya next time, buddy" his eyes glued
to the shimmering dress worn by Hector's mother

Waiting

Alphabet soup cools and
a layer of fat clouds over
words skim the surface
tilt the world and they slide off
like teeth or nails.

After surgery's unnatural sleep
from which I had not planned to wake
someone whispered in my ear
"a simple rearrangement...the body adapts"

When you go deep into your life
is it sand there and I am the sea
or is it sea and I the foam
crusting at water's edge
dry where once I glistened?

Waiting in the forest in the evening
or sitting in my kitchen drinking coffee
in pale light dreaming backward
I remember when a bird got stuck like some dark thought
and feathers scraped the wall like metal spoons

Now I mount the glossy bird
part the feathers and throw
my arms around the throbbing neck.
A red eye looks my way.

Last Night I Dreamed of Uncle Bill

who lived in back of
Imperial Beauty Supply
barred windows looked to alley
and the glass was painted black

Mirrored nightstands framed his bed
A hotplate warmed his food and
boxes of trinkets lured me to plunder

He loved a nurse with unsightly scars
and long-suffering Ida, who died alone
and his beautiful Marie, married to another

O he was a rogue my bachelor uncle
with ice blue eyes he charmed the women
but loved his brown dog Betsy best

He gave me a little diamond heart
Named his permanent wave the Saucy Curl
let me rummage in his treasure chest

From a clipping in the Chicago Tribune
"Solitude in the City" in black and white
my uncle stared blankly out a streetcar window
the lines in his face etched deep, his blue eyes gray

These Things My Father Left Me

My father and mother were linked like the teeth of a zipper
He carved a die to make her an ivory heart-shaped ring,
whittled a shadow box with intricate Chinese characters,
shaped me into obedience with the cunning of his hands
stained yellow with nicotine from Lucky Strikes.

He kept a blackjack in the nightstand
never never never to be touched
its forbidden weight heavy in my palm

Exotic friends ate at our blonde wood table
Geppo, the tattooed man: "cut here" it said across his neck
Chan-Chin who brought me embroidered silks, then disappeared

Dreaming of a Chinese junk
my father built a rowboat in back of the paint store
air perfumed with turpentine and amber linseed oil
I touched the artist brushes, sable, fan-shaped, precious
tubes of yellow ochre, Prussian blue, rose madder were my playthings

From the bottom of a boat I watched him steer us home
O, he could fish and he filleted white flesh
that sizzled in an iron pan, shore lunch
    "Never handle a living fish without wetting your hands"
    "Dread the fish that swallows the hook"
I trailed my fingers in the galvanized bucket
hoping for a kiss from quick dark minnows

He showed me how his hand
was quicker than my eye
My father, the trickster,
his lifeguard body still fine as he lay dying

There was a peach glow
the night of the lunar eclipse
the night my father was made to dust

He owned so little there was nothing left
    but the Northern Lights,
    the march of lemmings to the sea,
    the single day a Mayfly lives on land.

A Price Above Rubies

My parents were gypsies
a world unto themselves
Every four years they loaded
their wagon and moved on

They'd hit a town
Miami, Lexington, Beaver Dam
charm the locals, buy a farm
breed Simmentals
or plant fruit trees
rent land to Green Giant
During harvest they listened
as semis brimming with beans
zoomed past them in the night

Once they bought property on a canal near Cocoa Beach
Fixed it up, changed the name, sold for profit and left town
That was their M.O.: leaving things in better shape
                        than how they found them

                    *

When the space shuttle fell to earth
they found fragments on the beach
    moved away in stunned silence

One deal went bad----a building in Miami.... drugs
A week into ownership a body floated in the swimming pool
Next day they sold to a guy with a suitcase full of money

My father took to carving.
I watched Atlantic cod, mermaids and sea birds
emerge from the heart of old wood
He never liked to carve the same thing twice

He had a lifelong interest in the salmon
their struggle against all odds to swim upstream
their uncanny return to the spawning place to die

When my father left this life
an accident
my mother lost her ability to sing
couldn't even hum
She drew an **X** on her calendar
to mark the day he died
Black Thursday
Came full circle to Chicago
was welcomed into the bosom
of the family she had scorned
Each year she is invited to three Passover seders
two Thanksgivings and numerous Bar Mitzvahs

*

Today she called
Do you want that antique vase you called a helmet
the Lenox ramekins with gold rims I put hard candies in?
If you have a use for them just say so and they're yours
She got rid of the burgundy Buick
brought her silver to consignment shops
sold her ruby ring

"the miles are starting to rise rapidly . . ."

from Buckminster Fuller

End

When poetry leaves I dream of losing teeth.
In a summer without rain the cicadas are deafening.
Sunflowers droop like showerheads.
The sprinkler, on its rotation, sprays upward
blessing the underside of leaves.
In the past, the work sustained me
Losing ground, the body is thinning itself
the face, letting the bones speak.

Middle

We maintained the posted speed through tunnels
Sped past Willoughby Spit, Dr. Peppered our way
to North Carolina bought matching clamshell rings.

Sun rose out of water and a bird soared
Something dropped into my arms
smooth with abstraction.
I held my breath afraid of one wrong move.

In a cafe on the water fish sizzled in oil
a woman with teased hair and bright red lips drank sloe gin fizz.

A road sign warned "prepare for sudden aggravation"

After a biopsy a spider attached itself to me
When I tried to pull it off
it left teeth, black stitches at my breast.

When poetry went, it left me scared

I want to be in on the naming of things
have a house like Georgia O'Keefe
full of shadows and white bones

I collect the heart shapes, crescent shells, and moons.
I am told at hush of twilight seashells jingle in the tides.

The poets and the lawyers cannot help themselves
Each thinks the other ought to pack it up
do something real.

Beginning

I remember the in-a-door bed
how we rode it in an arc
swinging out of the closet on a squeaky hinge.

eggplant purple on the stove
burning leaves
grapes in a bushel basket
mice in the cream of wheat
and the dirty smell of my skin come in from play.

NOTES

Unless otherwise noted, these comments are from Bruce R. Butterworth

"In Fear." Written within days of the confirmed diagnosis of ALS.

"Not an Ordinary Flicker." Stanza 2, l. 4: Sauci questioned whether she should omit the line itself.

"The Red Fox." Sauci had a second title, "Meet it on the run." Line 2: I believe this refers to a friend who was so tired of being sick and in the hospital that he just left. Sauci was terribly afraid of hospitals—of their incarceration—more than she was of death. She suffered from ulcerated colitis between the ages of 16 and 29, and had spent about two-and-a-half years in hospitals at different times. She had seen enough.

"Not long for this world." A friend wrote: "Please tell Sauci I made a blessing for her at a Buddhist temple in Châu Đốc, Vietnam.

"Respiration." This poem was prompted by a neighbor's decision to cut down a huge, healthy tree that happened to provide shade for the bedroom where Sauci would spend her last days with me. She was upset, and asked me to talk with him because the ALS prevented her from speaking well. She asked me to give him a note with these Hebrew words: "Tikkun Olam"—"leave the world a better place."

"Seduction." The poem was impelled by the pain Sauci suffered—"who says ALS is not painful," she would say.

"Our Lady of Angels." Sauci felt this poem was integral to *Running Down Division Street* (2004)" but unfortunately was dissuaded from including it. Jewgirl was what she was called and it strongly authenticates what she experienced; also, "Dirty Jew" was what she was called in the event captured in "Running Down Division Street."

"Low Tide at Moss Beach." Sauci had an alternative to the last line: "a sliver of man's doing—undoing."

"Talisman." On the manuscript, Sauci had a note to herself: Tikkun Olam—to heal a fractured world; to repair the world—a core Jewish belief.

"An Artful God." Also known as summer snowflake, Leucojum is an adaptable spring-blooming bulb.

"Resolutions." Sauci had notes to herself on the manuscript page: "Body parts need maintenance replacement. At the dermatologist every little thing has ugly names."

"The Fireplug Unleashed." Sauci's "notes to self: genii of our neighborhood? Roman Mythology: genii were guardian spirits."

"Asian Carp." An inexplicable note in the manuscript:" fish scales magnify / the glistening/ wet eye of the deer."

"EgyptAir Flight 990." Sauci originally had the following epigraph but then marked it for deletion: *"The elephants went to the place where Lear fell, / all day … burying their trunks in the blood-soaked field."* Kim Echlin, *Elephant Winter*. The poem refers to the evening of October 31, 1999 when I was called in to manage the FAA security emergency center as Director of Operations for aviation security in the FAA.

"My Father." Sauci's father was crushed in the head by a spring of an automatic garage door opener in Florida in the late 1990s—he was helping a neighbor. He stood there with blood coming down his face. The medics asked him what day of the week it was—he answered correctly; they asked him the specific date; he said, "that's close enough." On the way to the hospital, he went into convulsions and when the doctors got him stabilized, they found he was brain dead. We released his ashes into the Potomac River. Later, on a vacation, she wept when she had been reading an account of Custer's Las Stand, how the Native American scouts had chanted their death song when they could see the Lakota and other tribes spread out below, saying "it is a good day to die."

"First Time in Paris." Sauci had an alternative last line: "His name is."

"Puppy Love" In today's environment the term "Chinaman might be objectionable but it lends authenticity to the poem, which clearly indicates that for Sauci the departure of this Chinese gentleman was mourned.

Sauci Sharon Churchill was born on April 25, 1940 in Chicago, and grew up in a working-class neighborhood, at the intersection of Division and Pulaski, from which she drew much material. Her first chapbook was entitled *Running Down Division Street.*

Her family moved to the northern suburbs of Chicago—a move she did not welcome for some time – where she went to Sullivan High school. She graduated from the University of Wisconsin in Madison, and took later graduate work at the University of California at Berkeley. She wrote authentically of those years in a neighborhood with typical ethnic and religious divisions, in which she herself was an occasional target. "Our Lady of Angels" is published here for the first time.

After teaching and working as a law librarian for more than three decades in a windowless inner core of a government building, she retired to work at Hillwood Museum and Gardens, where she asked only to be put into the light. She lived with her husband, Bruce Butterworth, and the third of their shelter dogs, Cloud.

In November of 2010, Sauci was diagnosed with ALS, and died of the disease seven months later on June 3, 2011. She was cared for every moment until the end by her husband Bruce Butterworth. Her daughter, Devorah Churchill from a previous marriage, mourned her death then, and now, as do so many of her friends whom she helped so much with her life, and her works.

Quiet. . ., which begins with the works written between her diagnosis of ALS and her last days, is published so that those poems will not be forgotten: Her husband says: "she faced death realistically, with unforgettable courage. She always chose her own way, and did until the end. I will always remember her."